Philosophy of the Mind
Made Easy

Philosophy of the Mind Made Easy

What do angels think about?
Is God a deceiver?
And other interesting questions considered.

Deborah Wells

BOOKS

Winchester, UK
Washington, USA

First published by O-Books, 2011
O-Books is an imprint of John Hunt Publishing Ltd.,
Laurel House, Station Approach, Alresford, Hants, SO24 9JH, UK
office1@o-books.net
www.o-books.com

For distributor details and how to order please visit the 'Ordering' section on our website.

ISBN: 978-1-84694-542-7

A CIP catalogue record for this book is available from the British Library.

Design: DKD

Printed in the UK by CPI Antony Rowe
Printed in the USA by Offset Paperback Mfrs, Inc

We operate a distinctive and ethical publishing philosophy in all
areas of our business, from our global network of authors to
production and worldwide distribution.

Contents

My Family

Acknowledgements

Thank you to John Hunt and the *O Books* team for all your hard
work and creativity behind the scenes.
Also loving gratefulness to my family and friends as we make
our way together through this higgledy-piggledy, often wonderful,
but occasionally downright challenging old thing we call life.
You are in my thoughts.
And especial thanks to Colin, Jack and Sam as I couldn't do any
of this without you

The rain continued to pound on the roof. Inside the shack it was warm.

"But you know there's a whole Universe out there!" cried Zarniwoop. "You can't dodge your responsibilities by saying [it doesn't] exist!"

The ruler of the Universe thought for a long while whilst Zarniwoop quivered with anger.

"You're very sure of your facts," he said at last, "I couldn't trust the thinking of a man who takes the Universe – if there is one – for granted."

Zarniwoop quivered, but was silent.

"I only decide about my Universe," continued the man quietly. "My Universe is my eyes and my ears. Anything else is hearsay."

Douglas Adams

The Restaurant at the End of the Universe (1980).

Introduction

Philosophy of the mind is a rich and remarkable subject. Its beginnings stretch back over 2000 years to ancient Greece and the works of Plato. It encompasses works by some of the greatest thinkers the world has ever known. It reaches into areas as wide apart and intriguing as ontology, mysticism, neuro-biology, consciousness studies, psychology and cutting-edge physics. What's more, by pulling you into its looking glass world, philosophy of the mind has the potential to completely alter your perception of yourself and reality. Philosophy of the mind is amazing. And don't be put off by any ideas you may have about crusty old professors, hunched in corners of dark studies, poring over ancient dusty volumes of impenetrably abstract philosophy, which they then discuss in terms that leave the rest of us gaping. Maybe this was once the case, but today philosophy of the mind is a dynamic and progressive area of study, and my aim in this book is to introduce you the subject in a way that allows you to sample some of its key concepts for yourself.

But first, a little about me. This is because the way we do philosophy, or the stance we take within it, is naturally shaped by who we are as a person: our background, experiences and beliefs. Some would argue with this and say that logic and only logic should provide the answers that we seek. However, every argument must begin somewhere, and that somewhere is usually within us: the stance we take towards nature, problems, concepts and the world around us. And this is one of the reasons why throughout history brilliant philosophers have come up with widely different solutions to similar problems, and you will see this phenomenon in action when we consider Descartes and his attitude towards animal minds. Therefore it can be useful to know something about a philosopher's background and to bear this in mind as you read their work. However, a word of warning: this can only ever help extend our understanding of their position; it should never be allowed to occlude the argument itself.

So first, just for the record, I am neither crusty nor old. And, second, I care a great deal about philosophy. Also, as I have just suggested, the stance I take towards the subject is necessarily coloured by my life experiences, and one occurrence in particular has had a strong influence on my attitude towards philosophy and philosophy of the mind in particular.

It began a number of years ago while I was undergoing major surgery. Before this time, I had been, so I believed, a fairly well educated rational individual with a firm grasp on what was and wasn't real in the world. However, during the procedure I happened to 'wake up' while I was still under the anaesthetic. By this I do not mean that I became conscious in the everyday sense of the term, for I had no awareness of the operating room or doctors. Nor do I think that I was 'near death', as such (though I never dared to ask). No, I experienced something far more puzzling – an alternate reality if you like, where I literally met the 'Ferryman'.

Now, I must admit that the Ferryman didn't have much to say: he simply refused to let me pass. However, it was on waking that the strangest things began to happen. Everything was okay for a week or two – very okay, in fact, for I made an extremely rapid recovery. But then I began to have *doubts* about what was and wasn't real. And the doubts intensified, stretched and snowballed, until I found myself caught up in a Cartesian-type descent (*see* chapter 1), which, over the space of several weeks, resulted in the gradual dissolution of my reality until I had *nothing* left. I lost faith in *everything*. I couldn't even trust the truth of my hand in front of my face.

It is important to realise though that, unlike Descartes, I never deliberately courted this sequence of events. It is also worthy of note that throughout I managed to keep my sanity and remain a fully functional member of society. However, my faith in the reality of the world outside me crumbled. And significantly, God and science were swept away equally.

What to do? I clearly remember standing by my bed one morning thinking that this couldn't continue. I had to rebuild my world. But how? Descartes had wheeled in God to help him, but God was not an option for me. So I decided that I would take as real the things which presented themselves as real to me: to my senses. It is a position which is, as you will see, by no means infallible (*see* chapter 3). However, it did give me the foundation to rebuild *my* world, if not the world in general. Yet it also positioned me as a sceptic, albeit an *open-minded sceptic*, which is the philosophical position I still hold today. And it is this that necessarily affects my stance, attitude and argument.

So what does this mean for this book? Well, for the most part, not a great deal, for you will still be taken to meet a number of great philosophers and explore some of the major themes in philosophy of the mind. Yet what is affected is the stance I take towards these themes, which is more neutral or open-minded than the stance taken by many philosophers today – though, again, you will see this for yourself as we continue.

I truly hope this approach will help you develop your own critical position towards these issues. Not everyone will choose to go further with the subject, of course. But if you are surprised by, want to reflect on or are challenged by some of the ideas raised here, then good. If you are entertained, even better.

At the end of the book I include a glossary of useful philosophical terms, and there are also some reading suggestions and addresses for those who may want to take things further.

Philosophy of the Mind versus Psychology

But before we continue, just a short word about the difference between philosophy of the mind and psychology. Psychology is a cognitive science. In psychology hypotheses are developed and tested under scientific conditions before findings are examined and reports written. Paradigms can and do change in psychology. Though, when this happens, it is generally as an outcome of scientific practice.

Conversely, philosophy of the mind is more concerned with concepts or themes, such as: *What is mind? What can I know about the external world? Is there such as thing as free will?* In philosophy these themes are not subjected to scientific methodology (even though scientific findings are often taken into account), but they are examined using analysis and rational argument in order to discover 'the truth'. Paradigms abound in philosophy. Yet the focus is on critical skills, which is one reason that philosophy continues to be a highly regarded subject today.

Chapter 1

What is Mind: Dualism?

Before we go any further, I should point out that it is impossible to study philosophy without *doing* philosophy. By this I mean that although it is possible to read the works of any great philosopher without really thinking about what he or she has actually written (ie. passively absorbing the content of the text), this would only ever be an exercise in reading or maybe general knowledge acquisition. However, as soon as we pause to consider what has been said, maybe to reflect on an interesting point or to mull over whether or not we agree with something, then we have moved from passively reading the text to actively engaging with it – and this is doing philosophy. What's more, one of my aims in this book it to turn *you* into a philosopher of the mind, in that, although you may simply choose to read through the text, you will also be given the opportunity to consider what *you* think about the concepts we shall cover. So let us begin by considering what 'mind' means to you.

....

Consider: What is mind?

Think for a moment about what the term 'mind' means to you. For instance, do you think that you have a mind? If so, where is it located? And what is it 'made' of? Is it simply a product of your complex biological brain or is it separate from (or different to) your physical body?

It may be interesting to note down your answers so you can refer back to them as we continue.

....

Have you ever thought about any of these questions before? If you have, you are not alone for these issues are fundamental concepts within philosophy of the mind and they have been analysed and discussed by some of history's greatest thinkers. So, to begin, we shall look at what one particular philosopher had to say about them. His name is *René Descartes* and he is widely regarded as the father of modern philosophy.

René Descartes

René Descartes (pronounced: *day-cart*) was born in the town of *La Haye* (now called *Descartes*) in France in 1596. He was a scholar, a mathematician, a scientist (points on a graph are still known as Cartesian coordinates) and a philosopher. In fact, Descartes' aim was to apply logical mathematical methodology to philosophical problems and he did this brilliantly in his famous essay *Meditations on First Philosophy* (commonly referred to as *Meditations*). Descartes published *Meditations* in 1641, a time when French thought was largely shaped by the doctrines of the Catholic Church which was quite hostile to the new science and mathematics of the age. So in this respect, Descartes was a somewhat controversial thinker. However, as you shall see, Descartes never truly separated science and God, even in *Meditations* where he set out to discover with mathematical certainty the foundations of human knowledge.

Meditations on First Philosophy

Meditations on First Philosophy is an essay in which René Descartes aims to discover what in the world is real and true. In this respect it is an *epistemological* study (epistemology is the area of philosophy that examines knowledge). However, for our purposes it has some extremely important things to say about the nature of the mind.

Imagine sitting beside a big open fire in a quiet study for six days while thinking about what is and isn't real and true; for this is what Descartes does in *Meditations*. Moreover, the way the text is written (in the first person) encourages us to join in the experience, and each day we are drawn further and further into Descartes' musings.

Yet, at the outset, Descartes knows that many of his beliefs rest on doubtful foundations. So, for once in his life, he wants to 'raze them to the ground' so he can begin again, anew.

But where to begin? Descartes decides to examine the information he receives via his senses. After all, this information forms the footing on which many of his beliefs lie. However, Descartes knows that his perceptions are sometimes mistaken, even though he is wholly sane. He also realises that what he experiences in dreams can be identical to his waking perceptual experiences; yet he has no real means of knowing whether he is awake or dreaming at any one moment. What if he is asleep now? His head, hands, body may just be a dream. Maybe he has no body. Maybe his perception of the entire external world is all an illusion. Therefore Descartes reasons that he cannot trust the truth of his senses.

Descartes then considers mathematics and geometry. After all, a square always has four sides, so surely he can take these things to be real and true. But then again, God, the all powerful creator, could surely make it so a square only *appears* to have four sides, after all God allows him to be mistaken about other things. But if God were good then why would this happen? So maybe God is a deceiver – an 'evil genius'. In which case, Descartes concludes, he can take *nothing* for granted.

So, here at the end of the first meditation, Descartes has reached the bottom of his sceptical descent. He can believe in nothing: not his body, his senses, nor even mathematical certainties. But then he realises that he, the bit of him that is thinking these thoughts, must exist. Thus whenever he thinks *I am, I exist* (or one of philosophy's most famous lines: *I think, therefore I am*) it is necessarily true. Therefore thought is the one thing that cannot be separated from Descartes. He is, he discerns, a thing that thinks. In other words, Descartes identifies himself (ie. the core of his being about which he cannot be mistaken) with his mind.

....

Consider: 'I'

Descartes used reasoning to establish that he, or the bit of him he refers to when he uses the pronoun 'I' to talk about his feelings, beliefs, doubts, etc. (for example, in the clause, 'I love you') is identical to his mind and not his body.

Now close your eyes and think about where you would locate your own 'I'. Is it in your mind? Is it in your body? Is it in your mind *and* body? Or is it somewhere completely different?

....

Two Substances

In subsequent meditations, Descartes continues the process of rebuilding his world – with a little help from God, that is (*see* chapter 3). Yet what is important here is what Descartes has just done: he has effectively split the universe in two. He has established that reality is composed of two distinct substances: *matter* (the stuff of the material world) and *mind* (the stuff that is real, mental and somehow identical to him). Thus Descartes has given us the philosophical viewpoint known as *substance dualism*.

What's more, it is important to realise that for Descartes these two substances – matter and mind – are totally different and separate. They do not intermingle for they have completely different properties. Matter, or the *material substance*, he says, has 'extension', that is, it exists within a three-dimensional space. Thus my laptop, the table it rests on and the cup of coffee beside it are all material because they occupy a space in the everyday world. So we can ask: What shape is your laptop? Where is your cup? How long is your table?

Yet on the other hand, the property of mind, or the *mental substance*, is 'thought' which does *not* exist within a three dimensional space. It is immaterial or incorporeal. It just thinks. Therefore it makes *no sense* to say: What shape is your love for me? Where is your feeling of joy? How long is your belief that the sun will rise? Unless you are a poet, but then you would be using metaphor and not literal language.

So the crucial point about Cartesian substance dualism is that it sees the world as being composed of two substances: the material substance, which has the property of three-dimensional extension, and the mental substance, which has the property of thought. Moreover, these substances are *irreducible*, that is they are the basic substances out of which all other things are made. They are also *separate*, in that the material contains absolutely no mental properties and the mental absolutely nothing material.

....

Consider: Are you a substance dualist?

Think about how you understand reality. Does it seem right to say that there are two basic substances within the universe? That matter and mind form the basis of all that is? That you, as you are sitting here reading this book, are made of a solid, if somewhat squishy, material body and an immaterial thinking mind? Are you a substance dualist? If not, how or why do you disagree with Descartes' position? What problems can you see with it?

....

Summary

What we have seen so far is that you cannot study philosophy without actually doing philosophy, ie. without actively engaging with the ideas and concepts within the texts. However, we can do this more or less formally, in that we can analyse arguments at a high academic level, similar to Descartes' logically structured arguments in *Meditations*, or we can simply consider our own thoughts and beliefs as we progress.

We have also met the philosopher René Descartes and looked at one of his most famous essays, *Meditations on First Philosophy*, in which he aims to discover what is real and true in the world. And we have seen that in *'Meditations'* Descartes splits reality into two fundamental substances: the *material*, which comprises the physical properties of length, height and width; and the *mental*, which is incorporeal and immaterial, and which thereby exists outside the physical dimension.

Chapter 2

What is Mind: Monism?

René Descartes' way of arguing changed the face of philosophy. What's more, his arguments in *Meditations on First Philosophy* more or less established the discipline of Philosophy of the Mind. However, not everyone agreed/agrees with what Descartes said. So, in this chapter, we are going to consider some of the different philosophical stances that people take towards the question: *What is mind?*

The one thing that connects these alternative positions is that they are all *monistic*. That is, unlike *dualism* which says that the universe is composed of two basic substances (matter and mind), *monism* holds that there is only *one* basic substance of all things. So, for the monist, the universe is made of either matter *or* mind – but not both.

To begin with, we shall look at some of the philosophical positions which take *matter* to be the basic stuff of the universe. In fact, philosophers who take this stance occupy a range of viewpoints, some of which differ significantly from others. However, for the sake of simplicity, we are going to group all these views together under the term *materialism*. And as you may guess, materialism is the orthodoxy of our time. However, as the book continues and we begin to look at some of the wider questions and issues surrounding the mind, you will see that the materialist position is not unassailable. In fact, materialism is plagued by a number of difficulties which are not easily addressed.

Then we shall consider the opposing view that *mind* and not matter is the basic substance of all that is. This position is known as *idealism*, and the philosophers who take it are *idealists*. As a matter of fact, idealism had been largely dismissed, even ridiculed, by many modern scholars. However, in my opinion, this is a hubristic stance to take, especially in light of what modern physics has to tell us about the world. However, I shall say more about this as we continue.

Materialism

Materialism is the view that *everything* in the universe is made of matter. That is, the stars are made of matter, planets are made of matter, oceans, rivers and trees are made of matter, and you and I are fundamentally made of atoms and molecules which group together to form the amazingly complex organisms that we are. Thus, at the most basic level, our blood, bones, nerve fibres, skin, eyes, heart etc. are 'nothing more' than countless electrons whizzing around billions and billions of nuclei. We are material beings. So, following this, materialism necessarily holds that our minds (if we actually have minds) are bi-products of our complexity in general, or, more than likely, of our vastly intricate brains. In other words, what we call 'mind' is an effect of the physiological processes at work within our skull.

Now I admit that this description of materialism is a bit of a blunt instrument, but it's a good-enough outline of how most materialists see the world – as a big mix of 'bits'. However, within these parameters there are many philosophical positions which we simply do not have the space to examine here. Nevertheless, we shall now take a brief look at several different materialist standpoints.

Materialism

As we have just seen, materialism is the view that the entire universe and everything in it is fundamentally composed of solid stuff, or matter. So mind is nothing more than a material process or the outcome of a material process. Either way, in a material universe, the phenomenon we call 'mind' must be *reducible* to material properties.

By 'reducible' philosophers mean that something can be *explained in terms of* something else. So, for example, if I have a headache, this might be explained in terms of tension in my neck muscles, which causes a tightening of my capillaries and other physiological changes, which in turn result in the pain I am feeling in my head. Likewise, if I am thinking about philosophy, or feeling happy, sad, angry or in love, in a material universe such thoughts and feelings must be wholly reducible to chemical states and electrical firings within my brain and body.

Now, as I mentioned earlier, materialism in its various guises is the orthodoxy of our day. Or, as the philosopher John Searle (1932—) says, there is a sense in which it is the unquestioned religion of our time.[1] However, as Ervin Laszlo (1932—) points out, this way of thinking has its roots in Newtonian physics, which is the physics of solid matter and the energy forces which act upon that solid matter; whereas new physics, or quantum physics, is uncovering a very different reality.[2] This does not make materialism necessarily wrong. But it does mean that philosophers should no longer take as given the truth of the materialistic stance.

Behaviourism

Behaviourism is a branch of materialism that is interesting because it flatly denies that mind even exists. This may sound like a counterintuitive or even bizarre claim – after all, we all know that everyone has a mind, or, at the very least, I know that I have a mind and I assume that you know that you have one too. Nevertheless, for the behaviourist this way of thinking is just plain wrong. And behaviourism was taken very seriously for a time. In fact, behaviourism had a significant influence on the science of psychology.

Instead of mind, behaviourists say that we have the *tendency to behave* in certain ways. For example, if I have a headache I may hold my head, complain, take an aspirin, etc. And this way of behaving, or the predisposition to behave in this way, is what constitutes having a headache and not any inward feelings or thoughts I may have. In fact, according to behaviourism, any mental-type experiences that I do have are merely *epiphenomena*, that is they are things which pop into existence but which have very little substance and no causative potential of their own. A famous example of an epiphenomenon is the sparkle of sunlight on water – it is there, sort of, but it does absolutely nothing.

However, as far as theories of the mind go, behaviourism is riddled with problems, not least the fact that if our mental-type experiences have no real value then why on earth did we evolve to have them? Also behaviourism takes no account of what it actually *feels like* to have a headache, even though most people would agree that pain is a powerful cognitive occurrence.

Functionalism

The final theory we shall look at is called *functionalism*. And although functionalism has some connections to behaviourism, it is a fairly modern approach, and it is sometimes associated with the concept of artificial intelligence (AI).

Functionalism is the idea that mind is defined in terms of its functions – the things that it does – rather than by what it is. Therefore a belief that I have a headache is the result of certain processes going on inside me which cause me to hold my head, complain out loud or take an aspirin. But the interesting thing about functionalism is that these processes need not take place inside my brain. No, if I had my brain removed and replaced with a computer, the same processes could, in theory, be processed within that computer and result in exactly the same outcomes. In fact, and again in theory, the processes could be carried out in almost *anything*. So if I had a fairy cake wedged between my ears, this small piece of confectionary might be able to run the processes which cause me to reach for the aspirin in an entirely appropriate way. Therefore although functionalism is compatible with materialism, it does not necessarily associate mind with the human brain.

Functionalism is an influential contemporary theory of mind, and there is a lot that can be said about it that we simply do not have the space for here. However, as we continue you will get an idea of how functionalism stands up to certain questions and issues within philosophy of the mind. Yet before we begin to look at these issues you may like to consider the following *thought experiment*.

....

Consider: Twin Me

Imagine there are two people: me and my twin. We are identical in almost every way. We wear the same types of clothes, we listen to the same kind of music, we laugh at the same jokes and we both drink coffee. Now imagine it is Monday and you are sitting down for a coffee with me. We sip our drinks while talking and laughing about the state of the world, and I happily assume that you have a mind which you are using while we chat, and I hope that you are thinking something similar about me. Now it is Tuesday, and you are sitting down for coffee with my twin. Everything is exactly the same except for one thing: my twin does not have a brain; she has a complex computer between her ears. She is an automaton, a cyborg me.

Now, although on the surface our behaviour is remarkably similar, would you still be prepared to grant my twin the status of having a mind – of being a thinking thing? If not, can you say why this is or is it merely prejudice? If yes, where do you draw the line – do all computers have minds? For instance, what about calculators which can solve mathematical problems better and faster than people?

....

Idealism

Idealism is the view that the universe and everything in it is composed of one basic substance and that substance is *mind*. However, idealism is a much maligned position in contemporary academic philosophy, and it seems that to come out as an idealist is tantamount to professional suicide. As John Searle says, 'Idealism had a prodigious influence in philosophy, literally for centuries, but as far as I can tell it has been as dead as a doornail among nearly all philosophers whose opinions I respect, for many decades'.[3]

Now, while I greatly respect John Searle as a philosopher, I cannot agree with this standpoint; partly because I incline towards the position of open-minded scepticism that I mentioned earlier, but partly because I think idealism is a concept whose time may have come again. Though, saying this, it is important to recognise that in traditional Eastern philosophy idealism is, and always has been, the accepted philosophical view.

Now, once again, I do not have the space to say much about idealism here. But to give you an idea of what it entails we shall briefly consider what can be thought of as its 'soft' and 'hard' versions.

Soft idealism

This is the view put forward by, amongst others, George Berkeley (1685-1753). Very briefly, remember Descartes' idea that he might not actually have a body; that he may merely be a disembodied mind receiving data about the world which may or may not be true. Well, as improbable as it may sound, this view is very similar to the stance taken by some idealists. For these philosophers, the only thing that exists is mind and all impressions of the external material world are simply ideas within that mind.

In fact, we all experience something very similar to this when we dream. For example, I may dream that I am writing at my desk, and in the dream the desk, my laptop and my cup of coffee would *seem* to be material objects; however, on waking I would realise that this was false and that the scenario was merely an illusion.

Likewise, think about how we perceive the world. We do not literally see, hear, feel, etc. the things around us. Instead we experience mental representations of things via our five senses. Therefore it is true to say that all we are ever aware of are mental impressions. Well, for some idealists this is all there is to reality:

mental impressions. The material world simply does not exist.

Hard idealism

Hard idealism differs from soft idealism in that although it takes the view that mind is the fundamental substance of all things, it sees this mind as being a conscious energy field which underlies all things and from which all things emerge. Again, you may think this sounds improbable. However, this is precisely the worldview that new physics is discovering actually exists. And it is looking increasingly likely that the 'primal ocean' of countless creation myths or the 'Akashic field' of Eastern mysticism has been re-branded yet again as the 'zero-point field' of quantum physics.

According to hard idealism, matter is mind made hard – the term 'concrete-ified' is sometimes used. And because of this, hard idealism has the interesting corollary that all things must be fundamentally imbued with some degree of consciousness – though not necessarily with sentient, sapient mind as we know it.

For anyone interested in hard idealism, the work of Ervin Laszlo may be worth reading. Laszlo is not an idealist, as such. Instead, he endorses the position of *panpsychism*, which is the view that both *mind and matter* are fundamental *within* all things. So, a bit like a magnet has a both a north and a south pole, according to panpsychism, everything has inherent mental and material properties. The philosopher David Chalmers (1966 –) also explores this view in his book *The Conscious Mind*, in which he gives a famous account of what it might be like to be a conscious thermostat.[4]

....

Consider: Are you an idealist?

What do you think of the idea that the material world is a dream or illusion? Do you think that the mystics and new physicists are correct and that our universe and all it contains emerged from an energy field or primal consciousness? Is the material world concrete-ified mind?

....

Summary

In this chapter we considered the *monist* perspective that the universe and all it contains is made of one fundamental substance. However, we saw that this single substance can be thought of as either matter *or* mind.

First, we thought about *materialism*, which generally holds that mind is located somewhere within the brain and that mental states are identical, at least in theory, to states of brain. We also looked at *behaviourism*, which claims that mind does not exist, only behavioural tendencies exist; and *functionalism*, which is the view that mind is determined by what it does, rather than by what it is, and we noted that this position opens the way for artificial intelligence.

Then we considered the *idealist* point of view that mind and not matter is the fundamental stuff of the universe, and we looked at two different types of idealism: *soft idealism*, or the view that the world is an idea or illusion, and *hard idealism*, which holds that the material world does exist, but that it emerged from a fundamental conscious energy field.

Chapter 3

What Do I Know?

In the first two chapters we considered the question, 'What is mind?' and we saw that it is possible to take various philosophical stances towards this problem. However, philosophy of the mind does not end here. On the contrary, now that we have a basic idea about what mind is, we can test our intuitions against a number of fascinating philosophical questions concerning mind and its contents. So, in the following chapters, we shall consider some of the questions that can and do occur to many people at different points in their life, and you may find yourself examining assumptions which up until now you have taken for granted.

To begin, we shall first outline a difficulty. For example, like Descartes we may reflect on the problem of what we can truly know about the external world. Then we shall consider some of the philosophical arguments that are related to the issue. Also, as we progress, you will be given opportunities to pause and consider your own ideas – for as I said, one of my aims is to get you *doing* philosophy as opposed to merely reading a précis of ideas and terms.

However, I warn you now: there are seldom any straightforward answers to these questions, for philosophy of the mind (like most branches of philosophy) involves an *ongoing* dialogue and exchange of ideas. So if you like your world to be black-and-white, cut-and-dry, then philosophy with all its twists, turns and infinite shades of grey may not be the subject for you. However, if you want to examine the foundations of your reality and possibly be challenged along the way, then let us continue.

The Problem of the External World
Stop and look around yourself, what do you see? Likewise, what

do you hear, feel, taste and smell? As I sit here, I see my computer keypad and screen. I hear birds in the garden. I feel the chair beneath me, and so on. Yet can I be absolutely sure that what I perceive is accurate and true?

This is the problem of the external world and, as we have already seen, it is an *epistemological* problem regarding what we can know about our surroundings. It is also a problem that has puzzled philosophers for centuries and there are a number of reasons why this is the case. But before we look at some of the difficulties, let us first outline what we mean by the everyday or 'commonsense' view of the world.

Commonsense Realism

Commonsense realism (or 'direct realism') is the belief that we perceive the world as it really is. Therefore, following commonsense realism, when I see my computer in front of me, the reason for this is that the computer is really, literally there. I see it as being a silver colour because this is the colour it actually is. Similarly, when I hear birds this is because there really are birds in the garden. And when I sip my coffee I experience the taste of decaf because, well, this is what coffee tastes like.

Commonsense realism is the view that most of us live with every day of our lives. It is largely the reason that we can function within the wider world. However, you don't have to be René Descartes to realise that this way of looking at the world is not one hundred percent infallible.

The Illusion Argument

As we saw in chapter 1, Descartes realised that the information he received via his senses formed the base on which many of his beliefs rested. However, he also realised that his perceptions could be mistaken. For example, on a hot day it can look as if the road ahead is wet. The moon looks larger and redder when it is low in the sky. A straight stick looks bent when it is half submerged in water. A man once asked my mother and me for directions, but she remembers him carrying camera equipment, while I remember him as a fisherman.

So even when we are wide awake and fully cogent, our senses can be deceived. And when this fact is used to argue against commonsense realism it is called 'the illusion' argument and over the years different philosophers have used countless perceptual anomalies to back it up.

However, it is possible to argue against the illusion argument, and one way of countering it rests on how closely we look at the things we perceive. For example, on a hot day the road ahead may seem to shimmer and move; but when I get nearer I can clearly see that this is not the case. Likewise, the moon is not really larger and redder when it is near the horizon and the stick is not actually bent – like the hot road these are merely illusions which I would see to be incorrect if I just looked closer. And as for the cameraman/ fisherman, well either my mother or I was not paying attention, for if we had been we would have both seen the same thing.

So although we know that in some cases our perceptions can be mistaken, on closer examination we do tend to see the world as it really is. Therefore commonsense realism can be thought of as generally true.

The Dreaming Argument

But Descartes had another argument against trusting the validity of his sense perceptions, and it was that he had no real means of knowing whether he was awake or dreaming at any one moment. Think about it, I may have a dream in which I am sitting at the table writing on my computer, and in the dream my experience may be wholly real and true and I may have no idea that I am actually dreaming – this would only become apparent when I later woke up. Indeed, there is a well-known phenomena known as 'false awakenings' whereby people wholly believe that they have woken up, got out of bed, even gone to work, only to suddenly wake up in their own bed with the realisation they have dreamed the whole thing.

However, once again, it is possible to counter this argument because for most people dream experiences are quite different from waking perceptions. For example, while I may dream that I am at the table writing on my computer, I may find it impossible to type what I want to write – and although I'm not the world's best typist this is not normally the case. Similarly, things may be wrong with the room. The sequence of events may be amiss. Or, more then likely, the feel of the process will be off beam or 'dreamlike'. Thus there is a difference between dream states and wakeful states, and we can usually tell the difference between them, at least when we are awake.

Nevertheless, the effectiveness of this counter argument does depend on the quality, vividness or realism of the dream. After all, some dreams, such as the false awakening dreams, are incredibly realistic and it could be that we care caught up in one of these dreams right now. In fact, our whole life could be such a dream. And this brings us to the third of Descartes' arguments against trusting the validity of our sense perceptions.

The Evil Genius, Brain in a Jar and Ongoing Dream Arguments

As you may remember, in *Meditations* Descartes thought about certain abstract or mathematical truths, such as the fact that a square always has four sides or that the angles of a triangle always add up to 180 degrees. But then he argued that as God is an all powerful creator surely God could engineer it so that this merely *seemed* to be the case.

This is known as the 'evil genius' argument. Furthermore, it could be that this evil genius is deceiving us regarding the validity our very world. Maybe you are nothing more than a brain in a jar which the evil genius has wired up to receive sensory impressions, so that you think you are living a life when what you are really experiencing is best described as an ongoing dream.

As surprising as it may seem, these way-out sounding arguments are not that straightforward to counter. For instance, regarding the 'brain in a jar' or 'ongoing dream' arguments, it is devilishly difficult to argue that if we are experiencing either of these scenarios that (a) we could ever actually know this was the case, and (b) this situation would not be congruent with life itself. After all, surely my life amounts to a series of experiences and memories of experiences, so, real or not, if you take these away my life would either change direction or simply never have been! Yet, even if this is correct, it does *not* prove that what I experience via my senses is valid and true. On the contrary, it actually verifies that I could, in theory, be grossly mistaken about the entire nature of reality.

Descartes himself made a case against the 'evil genius' argument, and he did it by constructing a complex logical argument. First he 'proved' the existence of God by reasoning that: (a) *the idea of God* has to come from *somewhere*, as you can't have an idea about nothing, so the idea of God must come from the perfect *Supreme Being* known as God; and (b) in the same way that being a triangle necessarily involves having the sum of your angles equal 180 degrees (anything else would be a contradiction, as if your angles equalled, say, 190 degrees then, by definition, you wouldn't be a triangle), so *a necessary condition* of being a *perfect* Supreme Being is that you exist (for if you do not exist then you cannot be perfect). Then he claimed that: (c) a perfect Supreme Being would be a *benevolent* Supreme Being, and that a benevolent Supreme Being would not allow him to be deceived. Therefore, Descartes concluded, God is not a deceiver; so he, Descartes, can trust that which appears clearly to him.

Admittedly, I have just summed up several of Descartes' pivotal arguments in a single paragraph. However, if you think there is something wrong with Descartes' reasoning, you are not alone. For instance, not everyone is happy to rely on the notion of God to prove the validity of a philosophical argument. Also Descartes' argument rests on his belief that God is benevolent, but if, say, certain parts of the *Old Testament* are to be believed, this is not necessarily the case.

Additionally, the notion that we can only have ideas about things which actually exist is hopelessly flawed, for example Lewis Carroll wrote about the *Jabberwocky* - a creature which is *not* real. And finally, and perhaps most importantly, Descartes' whole argument is *circular* in that he is relying on his clear idea of a benevolent God to prove that a benevolent God who allows him to have clear ideas exists.

....

Consider: A Brain in a Jar

Imagine that an evil genius really does exist. And imagine that however many years ago (around the time you were born) this evil genius had a vat of clear liquid within which he grew a human brain. Now imagine that one stormy night the evil genius passed a massive current of electricity through this brain (your brain) which was thereby brought to life, and that the evil genius then attached all kinds of sensors and probes to your brain which gave your living consciousness the *impression* that you were experiencing all manner of sensory occurrences, while all the time you were merely a disembodied organ floating in a vat of clear liquid. Finally, imagine that the evil genius structured these impressions to create the *illusion* that you were growing up, growing older, living a full and happy life. Now ask yourself:

(a) Would you have any means of discovering the truth of your situation?
(b) Would this situation in fact constitute *life*?
(c) What would happen if some brain-liberationists broke into the evil genius' laboratory and (i) communicated the truth of the situation to you, or (ii) eradicated all perceptions and 'memories' from the (your) brain?

....

There is one further argument against commonsense realism which, although not used by Descartes, adds extra weight to the idea that our perception of the external world may not be one-hundred percent accurate. Moreover, this line of reasoning does not rely on fantastic thought experiments, such as the *brain in a jar* scenario we have just considered. On the contrary, this argument is firmly grounded in contemporary science.

The Scientific Argument

What happens when I look at my computer? Well, science tells us that rays of light travelling at different speeds bounce off the object in front of me, pass through the lenses of my eyes, hit the light receptors at the back of my eyes, whereupon electrical impulses travel along my optic nerve to the back of my brain where they are somehow unscrambled to produce the representation of a computer in my conscious mind

Admittedly, how the amazing, technicolor, three-dimensional image actually materialises is still something of a mystery. Yet we can deduce that this basic outline is fundamentally correct by examining cases where there is damage to the eyes, optic nerve, orbital centre of the brain, etc.

However, one thing that we can be absolutely *certain* of is that we never, at any time, have direct perceptual awareness of the objects in our everyday world. On the contrary, *everything* we perceive is mediated through our nervous system. Indeed, new scientific findings suggest that in any waking moment we receive about 2,000,000 pieces of information regarding the world around us, of which we can only consciously process about nine bits of information at any one time.[1] Thus the commonsense view of the world is, at best, an indirect grossly partial representation, and, at worst, it's a subjective chimera.

Summary

In this chapter we considered the problem of the external world, ie. the epistemological problem of what we can truly know about the world around us. Mainly concentrating on the arguments that

Descartes used to question the validity of his sense perceptions, we tested the notion of commonsense realism by looking at the illusion argument; the dreaming argument; the evil genius, brain in a jar and ongoing dream arguments; and the scientific argument. And we saw that all these lines of reasoning challenge the notion that our perceptions of the everyday world are necessarily congruent with the world as it really is.

Chapter 4

Do I Have A Mind? Do You?

The idea we shall be looking at in this chapter is the problem of 'other minds' and it can be split into two different areas. First, there is the question of what sorts of things have minds and, second, there is the matter of how I know this to be true.

What sorts of things have minds?

The traditional or commonsense way of assigning mind is to divide the world into *inanimate* and *animate* objects. Thus rocks, computers, coffee cups, etc. do not have minds (they have no mental capacities). However, the sub-group of animate objects now needs to be split into *plants* and *animals*, with plants denied the faculty of mind. Finally, the animal group is split several times more with *lower animals* either denied mind altogether or perhaps granted a basic consciousness; *higher mammals*, such as dogs and cats, awarded further cognitive characteristics; and, at the top of the hierarchy, *human beings* with our fully alert rational minds. This commonsense way of allocating mind is not without its problems, however. And some of these problems are grounded in what we take mind to be. So before we continue, it would be useful to do the following exercise.

....

Consider: The non-minded and the minded
What sorts of things have minds? Make two columns, one headed the *non-minded* (things which you think do not possess a mind) and one headed the *minded* (things which do). List as many types of thing as you can think of in each column.

....

What sorts of things did you assign to each column? Which column was the longest? Was either column empty or almost empty? And did you include things like elementals, spirit guides, channelled entities, angels, gods or God on your lists?

The problem of what sorts of things have a mind is not at all straightforward, especially when we start to consider different mental faculties; though, again, we can roughly divide these into two categories: *sentience* and *sapience*. In this way, sentient beings are said to be in possession of consciousness: they are 'awake' or aware of the world around them and they experience sensations and sensory awareness; while sapient beings are in possession of knowing, understanding and rational thought. So, returning to the commonsense way of assigning mind, we can now say that lower animals may have a rudimentary awareness, higher mammals are probably sentient, while human beings are sentient and sapient.

In fact, this commonsense view of the mind is largely a legacy of the philosopher Aristotle (384-322BCE) who claimed that animals were sentient but not sapient. St Thomas Aquinas (1225-74) held the same view. Yet Descartes strongly disagreed with this idea for, he claimed, if animals have a mind then they must also have a soul. But as this view was in opposition to the Catholic doctrine of his day, Descartes simply denied that animals were in possession of even rudimentary consciousness. In other words, Descartes claimed that animals do *not* have minds and are therefore unable to feel contentment, fear or even pain. And, as nauseating as this may sound, watered-down echoes of this philosophy can still be heard today, especially in the fields of science, industry and blood-sports. Yet, even in Descartes' own time, some philosophers strongly disagreed with his standpoint. For example, David Hume (1711-76) though it 'evident' that animals were in possession of both sentience *and* sapience.[1]

Then again, if animal minds are not complicated enough, what about trying to assess what angels may be thinking about, for this is another subject that philosophers have considered. Actually, the problem of angel minds largely centres on whether or not angels are in possession of a physical body. For instance, St Thomas Aquinas and Roman Catholic tradition held that angels were purely spiritual beings. Descartes wasn't too sure whether they were spiritual, or spiritual and physical. While Western religious artists (such as Michelangelo and Milton) and the Bible maintained that angles were substantial beings.

Now the significance of this is that if angels are wholly spiritual entities, that is, if they do *not* have a physical body, then they will not be able to have sensory experiences, so they will exist as disembodied *sapient but not sentient* intellects. Moreover, the same applies to all other spiritual entities. For example, how can a spirit guide know what chocolate tastes like or coffee smells like if they do not have the sense organs needed to perceive these things? In fact, it is pretty difficult to appreciate what life as a wholly sapient being might be like as it would probably involve total sensory deprivation. A bit like being a brain in a jar *minus* the sensation producing sensors and probes, I suppose.

Finally, what about machine minds? Clearly, machines such as computers and robots are inanimate objects and are therefore non-minded, right? Well, not necessarily. If you are a substance dualist, like Descartes, you would certainly hold this view. But if you favour behaviourism or functionalism it can be difficult to argue against the idea that certain machines have minds. For instance, remember Twin Me? She had a computer, not a brain, but as her behaviour was perfectly congruent with a minded being, then the behaviourist or functionalist may have to concede that she does in fact have a mind.

And what of the idealist? Well for those who hold that everything in the universe has emerged from a conscious energy field then the answer is that *everything* – every planet, rock and cell – possesses at least a rudimentary awareness. Therefore, in this situation, machines – all machines – could be said to have a mind.

The Problem of Other Minds

Earlier in this chapter I suggested that you write two lists: *the non-minded* and *the minded*. I then hinted that one of these columns might be almost empty. Indeed, as we have just seen, if you lean towards the *hard idealism* standpoint, then you will have clustered everything in the universe into the 'minded' column. However, is it possible to do the reverse and have everything, or almost everything, grouped under the 'non-minded' heading? Well, as you may guess, the answer to this is yes, and we shall now consider two ways in which it may be so.

First, think of *soft idealism*. According to those who hold this view, the only thing that exists is mind, and all impressions of the external world are merely ideas within that mind. In fact, this view has a much wider currency then you may realise, especially in Eastern philosophy and so-called 'new' spirituality. However, soft idealism poses a number of problems, one of which is: *Whose mind is doing the thinking?* For instance, imagine that you and I are talking together in a room. According to soft idealism, my mind and my mind alone would be creating this experience. Therefore you are a figment of *my* imagination and *nothing* that you say or do can convince me otherwise. What is more, if I then leave the room, but you stay behind, you would actually *cease to exist* as you would no longer be an idea within my mind.

The view that my mind and my mind alone is all that exists is known as *solipsism*, and although what I have just outlined is a pretty strong version of solipsism, the fact remains that soft idealism can give rise to this problem. Some philosophers have tried to get around the difficulty, for example, George Berkeley (who was the Bishop of Cloyne in Ireland) suggested that it was God's mind that did all the observing. However, as we have seen, invoking the idea of God to solve an awkward problem – a tactic known as *deus ex machina* (god from the machine) after Greek theatre in which 'gods' would be winched onto the stage to help resolve a tricky plot – is a pretty unsatisfactory philosophical move.

The second way in which almost everything in the universe could be grouped onto the non-minded column involves a return to Descartes. As you may remember, Descartes argued that there are two fundamental substances in the universe, matter and mind, and that these two substances are separate, ie. there is *nothing* mental in matter and there is *no* matter in mind. Therefore I am composed of a material body and a mental mind. Moreover, the bit of me that perceives, thinks and passes judgement is my mind, and this is the *only* bit of me of which I have direct awareness. In fact, my mind is the only thing in the universe of which I have direct knowledge as everything else is mediated through my mind.

But what about my body, surely I have direct knowledge of that? Well, not according to Descartes' substance dualism, for remember: there is *nothing* mental in matter. So my body is 'nothing more' than an inanimate soulless mass, which responds automatically in response to other material stimuli in its environment. Therefore if I pick up a hot cup three things will happen: (1) my body will automatically react whereupon my hand will open and I will drop the cup, (2) I will perceive a sensation of heat and (3) I will make a judgement that the cup is hot. It is important to realise, however, that part (1) of this process is an involuntary automatic process occurring in my body, while parts (2) and (3) are mental processes occurring in my mind.

We shall return to the relationship between body and mind in chapter 7, when we look at *mental causation*. However, for now, the fact of the matter is that, according to Cartesian substance dualism, the only thing I can truly know is my own mind. I do *not* have direct knowledge of *my body*. And I certainly do *not* have any knowledge of *your mind*. That is, if you even have a mind, for it is logically possible that you may be a body without a mind, an empty body, a zombie, if you like. This is actually known as 'the conceivability of zombies' argument, and if I follow this line of reasoning then the only thing I could confidently put on my 'minded' list would be *me*. Everything else would be 'non-minded' or 'don't know'.

But wait, although I may not have direct first-person knowledge of your mind, I can surely deduce that you have one by watching your actions or interacting with you? Well no, I can't. For even if I see you pick up a hot cup, shout-out in pain, drop the cup and hop around swearing, I could, in theory, be watching the automatic physical responses of a mindless zombie and I would have no means of checking whether this was or was not the case.

Summary

In this chapter we have considered two aspects of the problem of other minds. First, we thought about what sorts of things have minds, and we saw that the commonsense view is not without problems particularly in regard to animal minds, angel and other spiritual entities' minds, and machine minds. We also saw in passing that the answers to these issues can be strongly affected by the philosopher's life experience and their attitudes and beliefs.

Next we looked at the problem of whether other minds do, in fact, exist. And we saw that soft idealism can result in the problem of *solipsism*, or the idea that my mind and my mind alone is all that exists, while substance dualism has the interesting corollary that zombies are theoretically possible.

Chapter 5

Did I Exist Yesterday? Do I Exist Today?

We are now going to look at the concept of *the self*. In particular, we shall consider the problem of *first-person identity*, which is the problem of when I say 'I think, therefore I am' or 'I love you' precisely who or what is the 'I' that I am referring to? Also, following on from this, there is the problem of *continuing identity*, for example, what makes me think that the person who appears in my old school photographs is the same person as the one who sits here writing this now?

The Problem of First-Person Identity

For René Descartes the answer to the question *Who am I?* was simple. Who he was, he claimed, had nothing to do with his material body for he, Descartes, the thing that he referred to when he said, 'I think, therefore I am,' was identical to his mind. Therefore time may pass, experiences may occur, the human body may change and decay, but none of this would affect his essential ingredient of selfhood: his mind or human soul.

....

Consider: Who am I?

Pause for a moment. Now say the words 'I am thirsty', 'I would like a cup of coffee', 'I love you', 'I think, therefore I am'. Add any other 'I' statements you choose and repeat them as many times as necessary, all the time concentrating on who or what you are referring to when you use the word 'I'. What you are doing is turning your attention inwards to find 'you'.

What did you experience? What or where is your 'I'? Is it your body? Your brain? Your mind? Your essential soul? Maybe it is located somewhere different. Do you even have an I? Make a note of your answers.

....

By now, it should come as no surprise to discover that not all philosophers agree with Descartes' hypothesis of the self. For instance, David Hume, who is widely considered to be the greatest philosopher to have written in the English Language,[1] argued for something entirely different. As a young man, Hume rejected religion and the church, and throughout his life his philosophy was marked by irreligion and scepticism. And the concept of the self, Hume claimed, is a mistake, 'there is no such idea'.[2]

This may seem a bizarre thing to say. However, Hume's philosophy is widely accepted as correct by many contemporary philosophers. Moreover, it is remarkably similar to the findings of modern science. So, to understand Hume, we first need to identify what is meant by first-person identity, and most people would agree that this involves an *ongoing impression of the self* which continues throughout life.

Hume then turns his attention inwards, as you did above, to consider where the 'I' is actually located, and he comes to the conclusion that, instead of an 'I', what actually exists is a *moment-by-moment* series of 'perceptions' which are run together by the imagination to form a single unified experience. So, for example, if I look inwards I may experience a feeling of hunger, of cold, of looking out of the window and seeing snow on the ground and so on. And my imagination then links these perceptions into one continuous stream of consciousness which I mistakenly take to be 'me'.

What's more, once the idea of personal identity is established, we then use it to bridge any gaps in our memory. So, for example, I might not remember my twelfth birthday, but I do remember something from when I was about nine years old. Therefore my (mistaken) sense of self bridges the gap and creates an ongoing impression of first-person identity.

Actually, Hume's argument is not too dissimilar from the way we see a series of still images projected onto a cinema screen come to life as a scene from a movie. However, the frames of a film flip by at a very rapid rate, so how long is a *moment* in our perceptual field? Well, if a person in a very dark room looks at a small image of bright light, and if they rapidly move their gaze across this image, they may perceive a juddery line of images instead of a smoothly flowing impression. So perhaps what they are seeing here is a discontinuous stream of perceptual moments.

However, this may not be the case as it is a mathematical truth that we all live for an infinite number of moments. So if a moment is a year, then my grandmother lived for 93 moments, but if a moment is a month, a day, a second, a milli-second, a billi-second, etc, then she experienced many more. And we can continue dividing time in this way, creating ever smaller moments of time, until we finally arrive at the mind-bogglingly tiny measures associated with new physics, whereupon, or so we are told, reality itself is created and recreated on a moment-by-moment basis. So a perceptual moment could actually be a minuscule period of time. Nevertheless, for David Hume there was no such thing as 'personal identity' as such, for he considered 'self' an illusion brought about by the imagination linking these moment-by-moment experiences.

Still, not all philosophers agree with Hume's argument that our idea of *self* is merely an ongoing illusion and it is possible to argue against it. For example, think of what it actually feels like to be you: what your own personal sense of 'me-ness' actually feels like. Now imagine what it felt like to be Mother Theresa, Henry VIII or Elvis. By this, I do not mean imagine yourself in their shoes. No, imagine what it was like for *them to be them*: what their sense of 'me-ness' might have felt like. You may agree that this is probably different from what it feels like for *you to be you*. If so, this suggests there really is such a thing as the *self*.

The Problem of Continuing Identity

The second problem of 'the self' we shall consider is that of continuing identity, though, to be correct, this is a problem that can be applied to many (if not all) objects that exist across a period of time. The story that is often used to examine this problem comes from Plutarch (48-122), with an additional twist by the philosopher Thomas Hobbes (1588-1679), and it is known as *The Ship of Theseus*.

....

Consider: The Ship of Theseus

Theseus, the semi-mythological hero of ancient Greece, had a ship which was put on public display in Athens. However, time passed and repairs had to be made (for instance, boards or bits of rigging rotted and had to be replaced) until eventually, not one single part of the original ship remained, every piece of it had been repaired. So the question is: Is the repaired ship the same ship as the one used by Theseus?

After you have come up with an answer to the first part of the story, consider the following twist. Imagine that every time a bit of the ship was replaced, the original part was carefully stored away. Then one day, these original parts were put together again to create a ship, which, although a bit decrepit, was part for part identical to the original ship. So the question now is: Is this restored ship the same ship as the one used by Theseus?

....

What criteria did you use to come to your conclusions? For example, did you think about the ship's name? Its distinctiveness? Its appearance? Its original components? Its ongoing existence on public display in Athens? However, if your answer to both questions was 'yes' then you have a problem, for Theseus had only one ship and it is an absurdity to suggest that two different things are actually the same object.

Now it does not take a massive leap of imagination to see how this same principle can be applied to you and I – to our continuing identity – for we know that our bodies are composed of cells which are continually dying away and being replaced anew. For example, on a cellular level our skin is replaced every two weeks, our liver every 300-500 days, in fact we have an almost new body every 10 years or so.[3] Moreover, you only have to look at my old school photographs to realise that the younger me bears little resemblance in appearance, tastes, cognitive ability and function to the me that writes this now. So how can I be sure that, despite all these changes, the person in those photographs is the same person as me now?

Well, as we have seen, according to substance dualism, I am my mind. Therefore any changes that occur to my material body bear no relation to my first-person identity, for the continuation of my mental substance, ie. my mind or human soul, is what ensures my continuing self. On the other hand, David Hume may say that any idea of first person identity is sham, and that that imagination and memory merely combine to create an illusion of selfhood and that proper consideration of my experiences would show this to be the case. However, Descartes and Hume aside, is there anything else that might support my idea of continuing self? Some things we may consider include:

- *Spacio-temporal continuity* – our bodies, although they change and grow, exist continuously across time. Thus there is an unbroken chain of material existence between me in my old school photographs and me now.
- *Cognitive continuity* – throughout my life there has been an ongoing process of mental activity. For example, an ongoing sense of what it feels like to be me or a gradual accumulation of new experiences and knowledge which are built on the old. There are problems with this, however, as there are gaps in my cognition; for instance, when I had a general anaesthetic or, to a lesser degree, whenever I have slept. Indeed, it is logically possible that at times

such as these my identity may have changed. In fact, one day I might wake up with a significantly altered sense of self without being aware how or when this occurred.

• *Memory* – we have seen that Hume thought that memory was a factor in our (erroneous) sense of identity over time. However, other philosophers, such as John Locke (1632-1704), have a less sceptical view and do indeed hold that memory is a key ingredient of ongoing personal identity. They say, for instance, if I truly remember events from an earlier point in my life, then the person that I remember must be the same person as me now. Yet there is a problem with this, for if I am using true memory to establish my ongoing identity, I first need to know that the memory really is true, that *it really did happen to me*. So the argument is circular, for I am using a true memory to establish ongoing identity, but I am also using ongoing identity to establish true memory.

• *Personality* – there is a sense that my personality (my likes, dislikes, attitudes etc.) has continued in unbroken succession throughout my life. This does not mean that my personality now is identical to my personality when I was nine years old. However, there is a sense that who I was then has changed and developed *one step at a time*, so there is an on-going concept of me-ness that links then and now. Nevertheless, there are problems with this idea for it is not unknown for a person to have a sudden and sometimes dramatic change of personality. For example, in *Zen and the Art of Motorcycle Maintenance* Robert M. Pirsig recalls how his personality was completely altered as a result of treatment following a nervous breakdown.[4] In the book, Pirsig actually refers to his earlier self in the third person, even though to the outside world he is the same man.

....

Consider: Mind Swap

Imagine that one day you wake up to find yourself in a different body – peering out at the world through a different pair of eyes.

Your mind has transmigrated while you slept. Would anyone believe you? Would you still be you?

We can look at this from a different angle. Imagine that brain transplants become possible and one day you wake from an anaesthetic to find that your brain, and thus your mind, had been transplanted into someone else's body. Who would you be – you or the other person? Whose identity would continue?

....

Summary
In this chapter we have looked at the concept of *the self* and at two problems in particular. First, the problem of 'first person identity', when we considered Descartes' idea that we are identical with our mind and Hume's argument that personal identity does not actually exist: that it is an illusion created by our imagination and memory. We then looked at the problem of 'continuing identity', where we observed the difficulty of isolating the criteria by which we can establish identity across time.

Chapter 6

Where Do I Go When I Sleep?

In chapter four we considered what sorts of things have minds and we saw that, depending on what philosophical stance we take towards the problem, everything in the universe could be said to possess some sort of mind or that I alone am the sole possessor of mentality. We also touched on different types of mental faculty; for instance, most of us would agree that higher animals are sapient, that we are sentient and sapient, and that it is pretty unlikely that calculators have minds – at least in a sense that would be meaningful or recognisable to us.

However, this brings us to another question: What exactly do we mean by the term 'mind'? For when most people talk about mind, I think that what they are actually referring to is some form of *consciousness*. However, the term 'consciousness' is itself problematic as it has many subtly different meanings. For instance, I may use it to mean:

- *Knowledge* – knowing about something or how to do something, especially when this knowledge is shared (eg. I am conscious of what constitutes a noun phrase or of how to work out percentages).
- *Foresight* – an awareness of what I am about to do or what my future holds (eg. I am conscious I have no lessons to plan this week).
- *Self awareness* – having a sense of who I am or a first-person identity.
- *Introspection* – being aware of an inner world of thoughts and feelings.
- *Phenomenal consciousness* – being awake to, or aware of, perceptions and sensations about the everyday world.

- *Higher-consciousness* – being awake to, or aware of, something that exists beyond the everyday physical world (eg. some people are conscious of other people's thoughts and feelings, or of ghosts, auras, spirit guides, angels or even God).

This is not a comprehensive list of the ways in which we use the term 'consciousness'. However, it does confirm that our idea of consciousness influences the things we think have, or don't have, minds.

For instance, even though calculators can work out percentages faster and more accurately than me, it seems that they are merely carrying out an automatic process – there is no conscious knowing involved. In addition, I am pretty certain that calculators don't have foresight, self awareness, introspection, phenomenal consciousness or higher consciousness. Thus, all things being equal, I would deny calculators the faculty of mind.

On the other hand, my dog has no mathematical skills whatsoever and I seriously doubt whether he has much in the way of foresight or even introspection. However, even though I have no means of checking his first-person experiences, I am pretty certain that he does have phenomenal consciousness. Thus I can happily accept that my dog has a mind.

The problem of sleep

So mind is primarily about consciousness, and consciousness is about being *awake and alert* to the world around us and within. But what about me? Do I have a mind? Well, I am currently thinking about philosophy and I certainly have foresight, self awareness, the faculty of introspection and phenomenal consciousness, so yes, it is fair to say that as I sit here now I do have a mind. But what about later this evening when I go to bed and fall asleep? I won't be awake and alert then. And I certainly won't be thinking about philosophy, experiencing foresight etc. Therefore when I fall asleep do I *lose my mind*? Or worse, if Descartes is right and I am identical with my mind, when I fall asleep or lose consciousness do I actually *cease to exist*?

The problem of the unconscious mind

Now even though dropping out of existence whenever we fall asleep is a logical outcome of Cartesian dualism, it is a pretty counterintuitive suggestion. Descartes recognised this, and his solution was to suggest that we are *never* one hundred percent unconscious, that there are *always* some thought processes happening, for instance while we are dreaming.

Yet although this may be true when we are sleeping – for example, most of us maintain some sense of personal identity in our dreams and we tend to retain a sense of time in that, on waking, we usually have an idea about how long we have been asleep – the same cannot be said for the absolute the loss of consciousness that (usually) occurs when people are under general anaesthetic or when they are in a coma. Indeed, these states are notable for their complete lack of conscious experience. But what is happening here? Must we now assume that the thought processes are occurring so deeply the person has no conscious awareness of them? That they are taking place within the *unconscious mind*?

Well the idea of the unconscious mind would solve the problem of me losing my mind when I fall asleep, for even if I am not knowingly thinking about philosophy etc, I can assume that I have slipped into a level of consciousness the contents of which are unavailable to my wakeful mind. Moreover, the notion of the unconscious mind would also solve the problem of me ceasing to exist whenever I stopped thinking, as my thought processes would simply continue at a level I couldn't knowingly perceive. However, as neat as this solution may seem, we cannot use the notion of the unconscious mind here, for it is, in fact, a *contradiction*.

Think about it. If the nature of the mind is thought, or, according to Descartes, conscious thought, then the unconscious mind must be 'unconscious conscious thought', which is a contradictory notion. Try it yourself - consciously think about a cup of coffee, now unconsciously think about it. This is, of course, impossible, not to mention nonsensical, as the contents of your unconscious are by definition hidden from awareness.

And it doesn't work saying that as your consciousness shifts away from the cup of coffee, so the idea falls into your unconscious from where you can retrieve it later, as you are now confusing the unconscious, which is hidden, with the sub-conscious, which is merely a holding ground for that which we aren't consciously thinking about at the moment but which we can bring to mind almost at will. Indeed, on waking most people's dreams are consigned to their sub-conscious. But, in contrast, deeply anaesthetised people or people in deep comas simply do *not* dream. They do *not* think. They have *nothing* to recall. They are *unconscious*. So, according to Cartesian substance dualism, these people must cease to exist.

The problem of the conscious mind

If the logical outcome of substance dualism is that every time we become unconscious we cease to exist, what about materialism? Does it entail this problem too? Well, if dualism can be said to have a problem with the unconscious mind, materialism has an even bigger difficulty because it cannot account for *the conscious mind*.

The problem here is that material things, such as brain cells, are quite simply the wrong sorts of things to create conscious experience. True, we know from scientific tests and personal experience that the brain is closely associated with consciousness. For instance, I remember one time when my horse refused a jump, I hit my head, and although I remained 'conscious' the world became very black with a lot of sparkly lights and I couldn't manage to speak for about an hour afterwards. However, the problem remains of how can material brain cells produce conscious thought?

Think of it this way. Materialists believe that there is only one substance in the universe: matter. And that matter is made up of bits: protons, neutrons, atoms, molecules, etc. And that these material bits are all there is to life, love and creation. So we can look out to space with the most powerful telescope and all we will see are bits. We can look down the most powerful microscope and all we will see are bits. And we can look deeply into a human brain and all we will ever see are *insentient material bits*, such as cells, nerve fibres and chemicals. Indeed, regardless of how deeply we probed, dissected or examined this unattractive grey organ, we would never, ever discover the colour red, the taste of coffee or the feel being in love. In fact, we could enlarge the brain until it was the size of a football stadium and then examine every conceivable corner of it, but, as the philosopher G.W. Leibniz (1646-1716) pointed out, 'we should not see anything which would explain a perception'.[1]

What's more, materialists can't account for consciousness by saying that as the brain is such an incredibly complex organ, consciousness just arises out of it, as this would be (a) returning to the problem of consciousness being an *epiphenomenon* and (b) saying that although one inanimate, material bit is not consciousness, if we place a billion inanimate, material bits side-by-side then consciousness will suddenly appear. The reason that this is a problem can be demonstrated by using Lego® bricks, for if one Lego® brick is an insentient object, why would a billion Lego® bricks that were fixed together suddenly develop knowledge, foresight, self-awareness, introspection and/or an understanding of the phenomenal world? They wouldn't, of course, as Lego® bricks are simply the wrong sorts of things to be awake, alert and aware. Likewise, material brain cells cannot account for conscious experience.

Could idealism be the answer?

So if substance dualism has a problem with the unconscious mind and materialism has difficulty accounting for the conscious mind, what about idealism? Well, if we take the idea that everything in the universe has emerged from a conscious energy field, then the concept of the conscious mind would certainly not pose a problem, for everything would be naturally imbued with some degree of consciousness.

However, it is sometimes argued that if everything has emerged from a primal consciousness, then why does our own consciousness stop at our skin, as it were? Why don't we have an awareness of the universe as a whole? But in answer to this it can be argued that our senses (ie. our phenomenal consciousness) overwhelm our 'higher' or 'cosmic' consciousness. And this is not a new idea, as mystics, shamans, Eastern religions and some of the more metaphysically minded philosophers have long argued that this is the case.

Moreover, there is a growing realisation in the new sciences that such mental interconnectedness is possible – consider the work of Rupert Sheldrake, for example. And Carl Jung certainly argued in favour of the 'collective unconscious'. However, some caution with interpretation is required here, as although in some writings Jung did appear to suggest that the collective unconscious exists outside and beyond us, his more orthodox approach was to view it as a biologically inherited predisposition of mind.

Finally, idealism has little difficulty with the problem of where we go when we sleep, for when we do become unconscious our phenomenal mind is temporarily arrested and we may simply fall back into our unconscious mind, or into the cosmic consciousness or Akashic field which underlies all things.

Again this is not a new idea, as mystics, shamans, etc. have long said this is precisely what occurs when we enter altered states of consciousness, such as trance or sleep. In fact, shamanism, voodoo and some other religious/spiritual/mystical practices (as well as, it could be argued, some branches of psychoanalysis) explicitly involve exploring and, in some cases manipulating, this underlying consciousness or energy field.

Yet in spite of all this, it must be stressed that none of these points make idealism necessarily true. They do, however, support the idea that it should be viewed as a viable theory of the mind.

Summary

In this chapter we have outlined two problems concerning the unconscious and the conscious mind. First, we saw how Cartesian substance dualism entails the counterintuitive notion that whenever we lose consciousness we cease to exist. Second, we considered the idea that materialism, or matter, cannot account for the conscious mind. However, we then noted that idealism, or the idea that everything in the universe has emerged from a conscious energy field, can account for both the unconscious and the conscious mind, and that this knowledge is nothing new as it has been known, and often utilised, in many different areas of mysticism, religion, etc. Yet it was stressed that this does not make idealism necessarily true. It simply adds weight to the idea that it is a feasible theory of mind.

Chapter 7

When My Mind Says 'Jump', Why Do I Jump?

The Problem of Mental Causation

In the previous chapter we saw that materialism has difficulty accounting for the conscious mind. That is, there is a problem in explaining how a universe that is wholly composed of insentient, *material bits* can give rise to wakeful, alert, conscious experience. However, there is another side to this problem, and it is that: How can something as insubstantial as thought have any effect on the physical world? Think about this. If I push my pen with my finger, the pen moves across the table. This action and reaction is, on the surface at least, reasonably understandable as the material bits that comprise my finger are acting on the material bits that comprise the pen, which in turn rolls across the equally substantial table. But what if I didn't touch the pen with my finger? What if I just thought about moving my pen – would the pen move in this situation? Well, all things being equal, no, the pen would not move because thought, or consciousness, is *the wrong sort of thing to affect material objects*.

Now let us move this thought experiment inside our own bodies and, sure enough, we can easily understand how one material bit, say our heart muscle, can have an affect on other material bits, in this case the blood cells which move around our body. Our heart beats and our blood flows. But could we make our blood circulate by just willing it to happen? Again, all things being equal, no, we couldn't as thought, or consciousness, is *the wrong sort of thing to affect material objects*.

Now raise your right arm. Have you raised it right above your head? Good. Now ask yourself how you managed to do this. The answer you give will probably be something like you *wanted* to raise your arm, so you raised it. You *thought about* raising your arm, so you raised it. You *intended* to raise your arm, so you raised it. In other words your mental state affected the inert, material bits that comprise your arm. But we have just seen that this *impossible* as consciousness is the wrong sort of thing to affect material objects, so how did it happen? This is *the problem of mental causation* and it is another central issue in philosophy of the mind.

Epiphenomenalism

Apart from the problem of how mind acts on matter, the materialist has to address a second difficulty concerning mental causation, which is that there seems to be nothing a body does which actually *requires* conscious input. We can understand this better if we think back to Twin Me, the cyborg me, who has a computer in place of a brain. Imagine that in addition to her computer-brain Twin Me also has a complex electronic wiring system running through her body in much the same way as my nervous system runs through mine. Now if *I* touch something hot, nerve endings in my fingers pick up this information and transport it via my nervous system to my brain, whereupon (a) I experience a sensation of heat and (b) messages are relayed back through my nervous system to the muscles in my arm, hand and fingers causing them to pull away from the heat source.

However, it is perfectly logical to suppose that if Twin Me touched something hot, messages could be relayed through her heat sensors and wires to the computer in her head, which would then process the information and send messages back down the wires to the muscles in her arm, hand and fingers which would result in her pulling her hand away from the heat source. At no point has Twin Me consciously experienced a sensation of heat, as Twin Me is not conscious of anything. However, conscious awareness is not a necessary part of her response.

Again, if I look at a ripe tomato, waves of light will fall onto the light receptors in the back of my eye and a message will pass along my optic nerve, whereupon (a) I will experience the colour red and (b) messages will be relayed via my nervous system to my lips, tongue, larynx etc, and I will say the word 'red'. Yet if Twin Me looks at a ripe tomato, sensors in her eyes would relay information to her computer which would process the information and send a command to her lips, tongue and larynx, etc, causing her to utter the word 'red'. Once again, Twin Me has no actual conscious experience of the tomato. But even so, her behaviour is wholly appropriate and comparable with the behaviour of a conscious organism.

Therefore what is consciousness if it does not have a causative role in behaviour? Well, once again, the materialist seems to be left with the problem that it is an epiphenomenon – a bit of extra sparkle that has no effect on anything.

Descartes and the Pineal Gland

The problem of mental causation is not restricted to materialism, as substance dualism also faces the difficulty of saying how an insubstantial mind can affect a material body. In fact, the problem is more acute for the dualist, as substance dualism explicitly states that mind and matter are two *different and incompatible* substances, whereas the materialist 'simply' has to demonstrate that mind is a property of matter. What's more, René Descartes, the father of substance dualism, was acutely aware of this problem and his solution was to utilise the pineal gland.

Descartes, as well as being a mathematician and a philosopher, studied human anatomy, and his investigations into the human brain revealed that whereas most anatomical structures of the brain are duplicated in both the right and left hemispheres (there are two temporal lobes, two amygdala, etc.) in the centre of the brain we have one pineal gland. What's more, Descartes reasoned that as mental occurrences are unified experiences, that is, as we have single coherent thoughts as opposed to simultaneously duplicated conscious experiences, so there must be a single point in the brain where mind interacts with matter. So, according to Descartes, the pineal gland has to be the point where mind and matter interact.

However, one major problem with this argument is that, even if it were true that the pineal gland is the point where mind interacts with matter, it still does not explain how this interaction is possible as the pineal gland is still a material organ and mind is still, well, mind, and the two remain mutually exclusive substances. Therefore Descartes' solution is no solution at all. In fact, the discussion of the pineal gland as the intersection between mind and matter is something of *a red herring*.

The idealist perspective

So if mental causation is a problem for both materialism and substance dualism, how does idealism cope with the issue? Well, once again, hard idealism, or the idea that everything in the universe has emerged from a single conscious energy field, has little difficulty with the concept. The reason for this is that, according to hard idealism, there is only one substance in the universe and, at its core, this substance is mind. Therefore in the same way that there is no problem about matter acting on matter (as in the example of me using my finger to push a pen across the table), so there is no difficulty with the idea of mind acting on mind, even if this concept is a little harder to visualise.

Indeed, mental causation is only a problem when cause and effect have to cross the substance barrier. So if there is only one substance in the universe, there is no barrier to cross, thus the problem ceases to exist. So long as, that is, that single substance can account for both mental *and* material properties, which is something that materialism, on the face of it, cannot do, but which idealism, if we can accept the premise that matter is *concretified* mind, can.

Summary

In this chapter we have looked at the difficulty of explaining how thoughts, wants or intentions can affect our material body. As we have seen, the problem lies in understanding how an insubstantial idea can have an effect on the cells, muscles and fibres of our substantial body as there seems to be no way across the substance barrier.

We have also noted that, in addition to the problem of mental causation, the materialist has to explain the role that consciousness has on our actions and behaviour, as it is logically feasible that an unconscious entity, such as Twin Me, could act and react to perceptual stimuli without having any conscious experience at all. Thus the materialist is once again faced with the problem that consciousness is an epiphenomenon.

Finally, we considered how hard idealism handles the problem of mental causation, and we saw that where the universe consists of one fundamental substance the problem of mental causation disappears, provided that the substance can account for both mental *and* material properties. So while materialism has difficulty accounting for consciousness and is thereby unable to answer the problem of mental causation, if we can accept the idea that matter is mind-made-solid, or *concretified* mind, idealism has no problem with the notion of mind acting on the physical world.

Chapter 8

How Important Is Happiness?

What is an emotion? What are they for? What role do they play in the way we make decisions or in society? These are some of the questions about emotions that are studied as part of philosophy of the mind. However, in this chapter, we are going to step back from these abstract areas of study and look at one specific emotion: happiness; as we consider to what degree we value happiness in our day to day life.

In fact, the question of happiness is more usually studied as part of political philosophy rather than philosophy of the mind. However, it is acceptable to examine it here for several reasons. First, most people would agree that happiness is a state of mind, an emotion, so we can legitimately explore our relationship to happiness in a book about the mind. Second, as many of you reading this book will be actively searching for a 'better' way of living and being, this chapter may help clarify what it is you are actually working towards. And third, by examining the question, 'How important is happiness?' we get to consider a fascinating thought experiment by the American philosopher Robert Nozick (1938 –). But first, we need to clarify what we mean by 'happiness'.

Happiness is...

Happiness is a feeling or emotion, but feelings and emotions are notoriously difficult to define or explain. For instance, think about a time you felt angry, sad or in love. Remember how it felt. Now use language in a straightforward way (ie. not using metaphor or simile) to explain the feeling to someone else. Impossible, isn't it? And this is one reason why we admire great poets, musicians, etc: because they use their skills to express feelings like love, anger and grief in a way that resonates with or is meaningful to us.

Through the ages philosophers have also attempted to define or describe feelings like love or happiness. They don't use the language of the poets, of course. And their focus is less on what it feels like to be, say, happy, than what actually constitutes happiness. For instance, Thomas Hobbes used the term 'felicity' to mean happiness, and according to him, '[felicity] is a continual progress of the desire, from one object to another, the attaining of the former being still but the way to the latter'.[1] In other words, Hobbes held that happiness is realised by achieving our desires, one after the next, forever on. So we might say that, according to Hobbes, happiness is *a state of being within the world*.

However, another philosopher to famously consider the subject of happiness was John Stuart Mill (1806-73), and Mill held happiness was simply 'pleasure and the absence of pain'.[2] Thus, for Mill, happiness was less a state of the world and more *a state of the mind*. So, following Mill, if I gain satisfaction by looking at a beautiful landscape, listening to a favourite piece of music, or being with my family, then this feeling would constitute happiness. Happiness is the sensation I have when I experience the things I like. It is not the things themselves, it is the feelings they produce.

....

Consider: Hobbes or Mill

What do you believe constitutes happiness? Do you agree with Thomas Hobbes, that happiness is gained through the achievement of desires? Or do you agree with John Stuart Mill, that happiness is a pleasurable state of mind brought about by the things we love or value?

....

I have no idea how you answered these questions. However, in the early 1970s Robert Nozick developed a scenario that allowed us to test our intuitions about happiness. It is called *The Experience Machine*.[3]

The Experience Machine

In his book *Anarchy, Utopia, and State*, Robert Nozick asks us to imagine that some super-scientists have developed a machine that, once we plug into it, will provide us with the life of our dreams. For example, we might pre-programme the machine to give us the experience of writing a great novel, meeting our perfect friend or partner, living a life of mystery, fame, adventure and so on. There is no limit to the good things that can happen to us in this machine. Moreover, we can periodically 'tweak' the programme to accommodate any new experiences we may wish to have. If you have seen the film *Total Recall* (1999), based on the novel *We Can Remember It For You Wholesale* by Philip K Dick (1966), you will have an idea of the power of this machine. Your experiences are indistinguishable from real life. However, let us add one further condition: once you are plugged in, that is once the electrodes are hard-wired into your nervous system, you cannot leave the virtual world of the experience machine – ever. You are hooked up for life.

....

Consider: The Experience Machine

You are given the opportunity to enter the experience machine. It is perfectly safe, you will be taken care of and no harm will befall you. You are able to pre-programme the life of your dreams and once plugged in things will seem as real as anything you have ever experienced – indistinguishable from real life. In fact, you will soon forget that you are in the machine. What's more, the programme is so flexible you are not committed to one single set-up for the duration of the experience, but you can, unbeknown to you, adapt things as you progress. It will be as if your life is blessed.

So, the question is, would you enter the experience machine for the rest of your life?

....

Whenever I ask people this question the overwhelming response is NO! In fact, I have never heard anyone say they would enter the machine and some people are actually repulsed by the mere suggestion of being plugged in. But why is this so?

....

Consider: Why?

What are your reasons for not entering (or for entering) the experience machine? Remember, there is *nothing* you can't experience in the machine's virtual reality world.

....

Nozick believed that there were three reasons why people would refuse to enter to the experience machine. First, he said, people want to truly *do* certain things and not simply experience them. For instance, you may want the satisfaction of knowing that you have worked hard to attain a qualification; applied your strength, stamina and skill to climb a high mountain; or to have met your lover's lips in a first kiss. And I think that most people would agree that a virtual simulation of any of these things, however realistic, would be a shallow experience when compared to the real thing.

Second, he believed that people want to *be* a certain way, or be a particular sort of person. For example, we may want to be intelligent, loving, kind and creative. Yet how can any of these attributes apply to an inactive, to all intents and purposes lifeless, body, that is merely connected to a machine? According to Nozick they can't. In fact, he goes further and claims that entering the experience machine is a type of suicide. It might even be likened to an insubstantial, meaningless Hell.

Finally, Nozick holds that anyone who enters the machine would be limiting themselves to a man-made reality which would be no deeper than that which could be engineered within a computer programme. The experiences may be realistic, he observes. Moreover, they may be constructed to give the illusion of breathtaking majesty or deep spiritual significance. However, this would only ever be an illusion of depth. It would be sham. There would be no deeper value.[4]

Personally, I feel that Nozick is correct in his evaluation of the experience machine. The experience would be a kind of meaningless, celluloid hell, devoid of depth, significance and value. But why is this the case, if while in the machine our experiences could be manufactured to maximise our pleasure and minimise our pain? In other words, to increase our *happiness* as it is construed by Mill.

Well, I suppose if our intuitions about the experience machine are correct, then we must conclude that Mill is wrong and that happiness is more than *a state of mind*. Indeed, if it was merely a state of mind, then we could separate the pleasurable response from the thing itself – that is, we could split the fulfilment from the study, the satisfaction from the climb and the pleasure from the kiss – and if we then synthesised the event (or created an illusion of it) in a way that created an identical emotional response, then the synthesis would be a perfectly acceptable substitution for the genuine thing.

But, as the experience machine has shown us, no matter how authentic the manufactured experiences seem, and regardless of how much pleasure we may be engineered to feel, most people recoil from the experience machine because, rather than a state of mind, happiness is, as Hobbes observed, *a state of being within the world.*

So detached happiness is not our goal. What we actually desire is to live within the world, to pursue our dreams and desires. And when we finally achieve those dreams and desires we will probably feel happy; though if we fail to meet them we will probably feel sad, or we may continue working towards them and find fulfilment, satisfaction and pleasure along the way, growing as a person and discovering deeper things about ourselves, nature and the world as we progress. So how important is happiness? Well happiness is good. It is pleasurable. And it is an important part of life. However,

I would argue that happiness has its limits, for more important than happiness *per se* is doing, being and experiencing within the world. What we actually desire is not a mental state, it is authentic life experience.

Summary

In this chapter we have thought about happiness. We first considered two ways of understanding happiness: Hobbes' idea that it is a state of being within the world, and Mill's proposal that it is a state of mind. We then tested Robert Nozick's famous thought experiment *The Experience Machine*, before coming to the conclusion that happiness cannot be separated from the object or action that triggers the emotion within us. Therefore, we concluded, happiness is not merely a state of mind, it is a state of doing, being and experiencing within the world. It is the actual fulfilment of our desires. It is contingent to a life well lived – to authenticity.

Chapter 9

Do I Have Free Will?

Imagine that you are strolling down a path when you come to a fork in the road. You stop. Should you take the right hand path or the left? Both paths look much the same. Both take you to places you like to visit. Indeed, you have no real preference for the left hand path or the right; you only know that you need to take one of these roads to continue your walk. So what do you do? You make a choice. You decide whether to turn left or right. But did you actually make this choice or were you influenced, programmed or determined to take one particular path, maybe long before you ever arrived at the junction. This is *the problem of free will*, and we shall be considering some aspects of it in this chapter.

What is Free Will?

Free will is the idea that I am able to choose what I want to do. We can think of it as the ability to 'make up our mind' about, for example, whether I want to turn right or left; whether I would like cake or fruit with my coffee; or whether I'll wear pink socks or grey ones today. In other words, free will is my intrinsic ability to weigh up my desires, reasons, motivations, intentions, previous experiences etc. and then come to a decision about which of these things I shall opt to do. What's more, based on my previous experiences, I am pretty certain that in situations like those described above, I *am* able to exercise personal choice – that I do indeed have free will.

On the other hand, I am not so sure to what degree my dog or a sparrow in the garden has free will. True, if I place a chocolate drop and a meaty nibble in front of my dog, he will eat one of the snacks before the other. However, to what degree his actions are 'free' in the sense that he applied conscious deliberation to the problem, or to what degree he was simply moved to act by instinct or appetite

I cannot be sure – especially as he seems hell-bent on eating both titbits at once. So, in this chapter, I shall separate instinct from the faculty of free will.

Finally, I also want to separate free will from the idea of 'political' freedom, by which I mean freedom within the boundaries of a coercive environment. For example, if I arrived at the fork in the road and was told by a policeman that the left hand road was closed and that if I tried to take it he would arrest me, and if I then I took the right path because of the policeman's threat, this could not be considered an act of free will. True, I would have examined my reasons, motivations, etc. However, a choice made under threat, force or compulsion can hardly be considered a free choice, so I shall not consider political freedom here.

So free will is my ability to weigh up my desires, motivations and intentions, ie. my *reasons*, against the options available to me, and to then make a free choice about what action I shall take. However, it should be noted that in real life free choices are relatively rare and that the boundaries between reason, instinct, appetite and coercion are often blurred. For instance, imagine that I get up one morning and deliberate whether or not I should go to work. I don't want to go, but I know that if I don't my boss will fire me and I fear this. Thus in this situation it is unclear whether my choice of action would be free or not.

The Problem of Free Will

Leaving behind the problems of instinct and coercion, we shall, for the sake of argument, accept that we all have an unshakeable belief in our ability to make free choices. We believe that we have free will. And we can test this claim for ourselves. For example, imagine that you are in a restaurant and you are handed the dessert menu: do you choose the chocolate cake, the fresh fruit salad or do you decline dessert all together. In practice, you would probably weigh up your reasons and then make your decision. Thus when we exercise our free will there is a kind of 'gap' between our reasons and our choice (we can illustrate this as: *reasons*< *gap* >*choice*) and it is within this gap that we deliberate, negotiate and manoeuvre. In other words, the gap is the 'space' in which we find our free will.

However, alongside our belief in free will, most people have a second unshakeable conviction which is that things happen for a reason. I do not mean, by this, that things happen according to some over-reaching principle of destiny or fate. I simply mean that most people believe that for every *effect* there must be a sufficient *cause*. For instance, pressing the accelerator in my car will cause it to go faster; gravity will cause an object to fall to the ground; or the earth's rotation creates the illusion of the sun rising every single morning.

We can imagine this like a line of dominoes toppling over: *A>B>C*... and so on, forever. This is the way our universe works. From the time of the Big Bang when all the building blocks and natural laws were created, A has *determined* B has *determined* C.... in one long unbroken chain. There is no gap here. We live in a *deterministic* universe.

However, these two unshakeable convictions create a problem for each other as they are incompatible. Think about it, if the universe really is deterministic, then there cannot be a 'gap' between our reasons and our choices. On the contrary, our reasons must actually *cause* our choices (*reason>choice*) in much the same way as my dog's instincts and appetites determine his actions. Thereby any impression of free choice that I may have is sham, illusion. It is just plain wrong.

Moreover, the idea that free will is an illusion is supported by practices such as hypnotism and Neurolinguistic Programming (NLP) which can be used to deliberately plant unconscious 'triggers' in a subject's mind. For example, a person who wanted to give up smoking may visit a hypnotist who may, while the person was in an hypnotic trance, plant the suggestion that cigarettes revolt the person; whereupon, on waking, the subject may find that the mere thought of cigarettes makes them feel sick, so they consciously 'choose' to avoid them. Indeed, some NLP practitioners hold that most, if not all, our 'choices' are directly determined by conscious and/or unconscious psychological triggers.

However, before we accept psychological determinism as true, we need to consider some of the arguments made against it. First, if it is true that psychological causes (eg. desires, reasons, motivations, intentions, memories) determine all my actions, in much the same way as my dog's instincts and appetites trigger his actions, then any idea of free will and the corollary of free will – *personal responsibility* – are thrown out of the window. So, in the same way I can't hold my dog responsible for his behaviour (I can only try to modify it by training him), neither could I consider another person responsible for their actions.

Therefore, if a colleague takes my pen, I could not regard this as theft as their actions are merely the inevitable upshot of their psychological determinants. Yet how far would you like to take this idea? For instance, would you be prepared to accept that Hitler or Pol Pot *were not responsible* for the atrocities which occurred under their regimes? Most people balk at the idea of allowing such people to waive responsibility for their choices and actions, but this would be the inevitable consequence if psychological determinism were true.

Second, if psychological determinism is true, then I have to regard my unshakable belief that I have free will as false. I am wrong. My conviction that I have any sort of freedom to choose is mistaken. And no matter what I do or how cleverly I try to choose, I would have to accept that any sense of personal freedom I may have is illusory.

Again, this is an unacceptable conclusion for most people. However, it brings us to a third problem with psychological determinism, which is, if psychological determinism is true, then why have we evolved to possess this unshakeable sense of our own ability to choose? For sure, it is hard to see how such a conviction could possibly give us the evolutionary edge over, say, an ape acting on pure instinct. In fact, it would probably be an evolutionary *disadvantage*, as the ape acting on instinct would act more swiftly and decisively than a deliberating human – unless, that is, free will is actually true.

Finally, if psychological determinism is true, then it must be true in *every* case and for *all* my choices. For instance, I can't say, 'Well yes, some of my decisions are determined by psychological triggers, but this isn't true in the case of, say, my decision to have chocolate cake instead of fresh fruit salad'. If my choices are psychologically determined, then my choices are jolly well psychologically determined, and I can't hop and skip between determinism and freedom of choice as I please. Unless, that is, my mind operates on different principles to everything else in the universe, in which case it must exist, at least in part, outside of three dimensional space. In other words, my mind would need to be a different type of *thing* to my material body – which essentially brings us back to Cartesian substance dualism.

On the other hand, you may be wondering how idealism stands up to the concept of free will, but I can tell you now that the answer is not too well. The problem, you see, isn't between materialism and idealism, for if the fundamental substance of the universe is mind, then mind would be the fundamental determinant. And although this might help remove some abstract boundary between psychological and regular determinism, it can't explain how or why we have this unshakeable belief in our own ability to choose; for determinism is determinism and, no matter how we package it, it remains incompatible with the idea of free will. Indeed, the real difficulty in this situation lies solely between the concepts of determinism and freedom of choice, for, as we have seen, unless mind is a different kind of thing to matter (ie. a different kind of substance) it seems that one of these unshakeable convictions must be wrong.

Summary

In this chapter we have seen that most people have two unshakeable beliefs regarding the nature of the universe: (a) that things happen for a reason, or that for every effect there must be a sufficient cause, and (b) that human beings have free will. Yet we noted that these two principles are incompatible, and that this is equally true whether we hold matter or mind to be the basic stuff of the universe. Indeed, we saw that for both convictions to be true, mind would have to be a different type of thing to everything else in the universe and to exist, at least in part, outside of three-dimensional space – an idea which takes us back to Cartesian substance dualism.

Chapter 10

Can I Survive Death?

One of the largest questions to concern any of us is: What happens when we die? Some say that immortality awaits us in Paradise. Some that we will ascend to blessed Heaven. Others claim that we will be reborn, perhaps again and again in an ongoing cycle, maybe as ourselves, or as another person, or possibly not even as a human being. Then there are those who believe that in the afterlife things continue pretty much as they did before we died, except that we will be young again and free from ailment or injury. While others say that after death we ascend through different levels of heaven, some of which possess a comforting homeliness and some of which contain vast schools of learning. Yet it may also be that nothing positive awaits us and instead we may find ourselves roasting in a fiery inferno, freezing in a in a bitter Hell or whiling away our forevers in some dark shadowland of the soul. Then again, perhaps nothing happens at all. Maybe when the lights go out in our eyes at the end of our life we simply cease to be.

In fact, most people hold some sort of belief regarding what happens to a person or personality after their death. Moreover, some people go still further and say that *belief* doesn't come into this and that they *know* what lies on the other side. Problematically, though, believers and non-believers alike can take this dogmatic stance – which means that somebody must be wrong. However, while I try to respect everyone's beliefs, and while there are certain people I sincerely admire who hold some very strong ideas about the afterlife, for my part I have to say that I don't know what to think – I am open minded.

This doesn't mean, however, that I never think about the problem, for the concept of life after death is very closely associated with the mind-body problem that we considered at the beginning of the book, when we thought about whether the basic stuff of the universe is matter, mind, or matter and mind. In fact, what we take mind to be can, to a large degree, shape or define our belief about what happens to us when we die. Likewise, the opposite is also true in that our strongly held beliefs about death can, and often do, shape our thinking about the nature of the mind.

....

Consider: What Happens To Us When We Die?

Think for a while about your own beliefs about what happens to a person after they die. Do you have a clear idea about what *you think* happens or are your ideas jumbled? Try to clarify your thoughts as much as possible. Now think about your ideas concerning mind. Would you say you are a substance dualist, a materialist, an idealist? Or maybe you lean towards one of the other positions we looked at more briefly, such as functionalism or panpsychism.

Consider how your beliefs about death and mind correlate. Can you see how they may support or contradict one another? Try to think of answers to any potential problems.

....

Death and the mind-body problem

So what happens to us when we die? Well, for the substance dualist the answer would seem to be reasonably straightforward in that when the body dies the mind or 'soul' becomes liberated from the material world. However, even if we assume that the mind can exist without a body, it is by no means certain that a *personality* could have a separate existence, as so much of who we are 'on the inside' is bound to who we are 'on the outside'.

For example, my sense of identity is pretty closely related to how I look, what I like, what I dislike, what I enjoy doing and so on. Therefore, if we take away the stuff that is related to the material body, what do we have left? To me, it seems that my bodiless mind wouldn't be a million miles removed from an angel mind in that I would simply be a thing that thinks: a sapient entity whose existence merely entails pure thought. True, I may remember for a while what a kiss felt like or how music sounded, but without continual reinforcement these memories would soon fade until all I would be left with is the faculty of logical thought.

Also it is by no means certain that I would be able to perceive other spirits or, even if I could 'see' them, that I would be able to communicate with them. I suppose I might use telepathy, yet there is no guarantee that this would be possible. In fact, it seems that for a disembodied mind, the afterlife may be very close to being a brain in a jar – minus the sense-producing electrodes. In other words, a very *lonely* existence (*see* chapter 4).

Yet maybe this is preferable to the materialist's idea of the afterlife which is, on the face of it, non existent, as when the material body dies, the mind, which is a part of that body, must die also. However, this does not necessarily follow. For, as no one is entirely sure what mind is, how it is generated within the body or even how it stored, say in the form of memories, it is impossible to be certain that mind is simply 'snuffed out' at the end of life. For sure, there have been accounts of people who have received organ transplants suddenly acquiring the memories, tastes and even personality traits of the deceased donor.

And what if mind is a feature of lower level physiology? What if it is held on a cellular or even an atomic level? Such an idea would not be at odds with materialism. And there is little doubt that the atoms and molecules which now comprise me will one day find their way into new life via the soil, air and water.

In fact, it may be that mind regularly finds its way back into new life, though how this might happen and what it could entail is again open to question. For instance, it may be that a disembodied mind (or soul) hovers around until it finds a suitable foetus to occupy – though at what stage this 'possession' takes place is unclear, with different people claiming that the soul enters the body at conception, during gestation, immediately prior to delivery, during delivery or in the hours and days following birth.

However, even if we could pinpoint *when* mind connects with the body, we are then left with the problem of *how* this process actually takes place. And there are similarities here to the problem Descartes faced when he tried to explain how mind and body are connected and how they interact (*see* chapter 7).

Yet, even if we knew *when* and *how* body and mind came together, we would still have to think about the problem of continuing identity. For, as being 'born again' typically involves being reincarnated into a new body; possibly having a different gender, race, culture, class and creed; and almost certainly losing all conscious memory of any previous existence(s), it seems difficult to see in what sense *I* have survived.

This problem is closely related to the problem of *The Ship of Theseus* (*see* chapter 5), in that we need to determine precisely which criteria establish continuing identity. However, as all the things that define *me* are apparently bound up with my *personality*, which as we saw above cannot survive in the afterlife, then all that remains is the remote, logical, personality-less aspect of mind that could, in theory, exist in jar.

And this may indeed be my essential soul. However, it most certainly is not *me, I, Debbie*, in any sense that I would actually recognise. Therefore, even if this aloof piece of mind can and does find its way back into life, I cannot accept that *I* will actually survive.

On the other hand, if I were an idealist I might say that at the time of death, when all my bodily functions cease, my material body will gradually begin to decay to the dust from whence it came, but that my mind (in whole or in part) will still be contained within that dust (ie. in the molecules and atoms that once comprised me). This is a theory which would offer some explanation as to why transplant patients can apparently acquire the donor's traits and tastes. Nevertheless, an idealist may also claim that at the time of death, my mind will be absorbed back into the universal consciousness/

Akashic field/zero point field (or whatever else we may choose to call the sea of consciousness which underlies all life and being). And if this is the case, then although I myself will not necessarily survive, all my thoughts, memories and perceptual experiences will continue to exist: recorded in the universal consciousness.

What's more, this outcome may offer an explanation for what are sometimes termed 'past life' memories, as a sufficiently sensitive person or someone in an altered state of consciousness may be able to tune into these universal memories, which they may interpret as belonging to their own history.

Summary

In this chapter we have thought about how mind, and our idea of mind, is intimately connected to our conception of death. It is important to realise, though, that the aim of the chapter is not to destroy anyone's personal beliefs, for, with an absence of direct evidence, how can *anyone* be completely sure what really happens when we die? Also, as I have already mentioned, I am open minded about such things; and, as an open minded person, I have to acknowledge that sometimes people have strange experiences which cannot be explained by the tenets of everyday logic and/or science (my experience under anaesthetic being one such example), so they naturally look for explanations elsewhere. What's more, some of the things we have considered in this chapter, such as the Akashic field or transmigration, do provide an explanation for at least some of these events. Yet whether this amounts to irrefutable proof for the existence of, say, past lives, I can't be sure, for it could 'simply' be that my mind has created these strange occurrences.

Indeed, one thing that I *am* certain of is that the human mind is a vastly complex substance/organ/phenomenon which is capable of some amazing, strange and baffling things that science can barely begin to understand. However, as philosophers we are not limited by the constraints of science (even though we might use scientific knowledge to further our understanding), so we shall continue thinking, questioning and probing the mysteries of the mind until we finally arrive at 'the truth'.

Taking It Further

So here we are at the end of the book and I hope that you have enjoyed reading, and indeed thinking, about some of the ideas and concepts studied in *philosophy of the mind*. Of course, no book can hope to cover everything about this area of philosophy. Indeed, most philosophers focus on just a few of the topics covered here, maybe concentrating their efforts on the nature of consciousness, free will or the problem of what we can actually know. However, the *Made Easy* approach has allowed us to cover a lot of ground very quickly, and has given us the opportunity to look at a number of philosophers and philosophical problems, and to do some philosophy along the way. Indeed, after considering some of the questions and issues raised here, you may now be thinking that *nothing* is a straightforward as it initially seems.

I would also like to think that you have found at least some of the areas we have covered inherently interesting. But I'm also guessing that you will have disagreed with various points or felt frustration at that which was omitted. That's okay. That's philosophy. For as I said at the beginning of this book, philosophy doesn't deal in absolute answers. Instead, it's an ongoing dialogue, sometimes stretching back millennia, between people who *think* about the world around themselves and within. So if you are one of those thinking people, and if you feel like taking things a little further, there are a number of options available to you.

Books

There are any number of books available covering many different branches of philosophy. However, philosophy books range from the very accessible to the bafflingly esoteric, with just about every base covered in between. But don't assume that material written by the late greats of philosophy, such as Descartes or Hume, is necessarily more difficult than that written by contemporary philosophers. On the contrary, some of these classic works have stood the test of time for a good reason – they are beautifully written. So please don't shy away from reading titles such as *Meditations on First Philosophy*, just choose a copy with some good editor's notes to guide you, and that has been published by a respected publisher. I like the *Oxford Philosophical Texts* series, published by Oxford University Press; *Hackett* philosophy books, published by Hackett Publishing Company; the *Oxford World Classics* series, published by Oxford University Press; and the *Penguin Classics* series, published by Penguin Books. This is not a complete list, of course, but if I was looking for a classic text I would probably begin by checking what these publishers had available. For contemporary philosophical texts the picture widens somewhat, but some good modern classics are mentioned in the reference section of this book.

Study

For anyone who would like to take the study of philosophy even further there are a number of opportunities. For instance, many local adult education programmes offer day and / or evening classes in philosophy. Alternatively, if you are interested distance learning, you could study for a GCE in the subject with the *National Extension College* (NEC), while the *Open University* (OU) offers graduate and post-graduate level courses. Some of these options are not cheap, however, as you will be a fee-paying student. But both the NEC and the OU offer financial assistance to students who meet the correct academic and financial criteria. Also, both NEC and OU courses are available to students in many countries outside the UK.

The National Extension College
Michael Young Centre, Purbeck Road, Cambridge, CB2 2HN
Tel: +44 (0)1223 400200
www.nec.ac.uk

The Open University (UK)
Walton Hall, Milton Keynes, MK7 6AA
Tel: +44 (0)845 300 60 90
www.open.ac.uk

References

Chapter 2
What Is Mind: Monism?
[1] Searle, J.R. (2004) *Mind: A Brief Introduction*, New York, Oxford University Press.
[2] Laszlo. E, (2004, 2007) *Science and the Akashic Field: An Integral Theory of Everything*, Vermont, Inner Traditions.
[3] Searle, J.R. (2004) *Mind: A Brief Introduction*, New York, Oxford University Press.
[4] Chalmers, D. (1986) *The Conscious Mind: In Search of a Fundamental Theory*, Oxford, Oxford University Press.

Chapter 3
What Do I Know?
[1] Mayne, B. (2006) *Goal Mapping: A Practical Workbook*, London, Watkins.

Chapter 4
Do I Have A Mind? Do You?
[1] Hume. D. (2000) *A Treatise on Human Nature*, Norton, D.F. and Norton, M.J. (eds.) Oxford, Oxford University Press.

Chapter 5
Did I Exist Yesterday? Do I Exist Today?
[1] Mautner, N. (ed) (2000) *The Penguin Dictionary of Philosophy*, London, Penguin Books.
[2] Hume. D. (2000) *A Treatise on Human Nature*, Norton, D.F. and Norton, M.J. (eds.) Oxford, Oxford University Press.
[3] Wade, N. (2005) *Your Body is Younger than You Think*, [online], N.Y. New York Times. Available from: http://www.nytimes.com/2005/08/02/science/02cell.html (Accessed 10 January 2010)
[4] Pirsig, R.M. (1974) *Zen and the Art of Motorcycle Maintenance*, London, Vintage.

Chapter 6
Where Do I Go When I Sleep?

[1] Leibniz, G.W. (1973) *Philosophical Writings*, London, Dent.

Chapter 8
How Important Is Happiness?

[1] Hobbes, T. (1994) *Leviathan*, Curley, E. (ed), Indianapolis, Hackett Publishing Company, Inc.

[2] Mill, J.S. (1998) *Utilitarianism*, Crisp, R (ed), Oxford, Oxford University Press.

[3] Nozick, R. (1978) *Anarchy, State, and Utopia*, Oxford, Blackwell.

[4] Nozick, R. (1978) *Anarchy, State, and Utopia*, Oxford, Blackwell.

Glossary

Behaviourism – A theory which claims that mind does not exist: only behavioural tendencies exist.

Cartesian – Relating to the theories of the philosopher *René Descartes*.

Circular Argument – An argument that uses *A* to explain *B*, and *B* to explain *A*. In other words, an argument that doesn't actually tell us anything.

Concretified – The name of the process by which immaterial mind becomes solid matter.

Commonsense Realism – The idea that we perceive the world as it really is.

Contradiction – Two ideas which cannot both be right as one opposes or denies the other.

Determinism – The process by which every event in the universe has an antecedent cause (ie. cause and effect).

Deus ex machina – Using the concept of God to resolve a complicated logical problem.

Dualism – The idea that the universe is composed of two basic substances: matter *and* mind.

Epistemology – The study of what we can and/or do know.

Functionalism – A theory which defines mind by what it *does*, rather than by what it *is*.

Idealism – The theory that mind is the fundamental substance of all that is.

Materialism – The theory that matter is the fundamental substance of all that is.

Material Substance – The basic three-dimensional stuff of which the material universe is made.

Mental Substance – The basic stuff of the immaterial thinking mind.

Monism – The idea that the universe is composed of one basic substance: matter *or* mind.

Panpsychism – The theory that *mind and matter* are fundamental within all things.

Paradigm – A set of attitudes, beliefs, thoughts, opinions, etc. that create a particular way of thinking and / or being.

Qualia – The essential qualities of the things we perceive, eg. the particular redness of a tomato.

Red Herring – An idea or concept that is distracting or irrelevant.

Scepticism – The idea that we don't / can't know anything with any certainty.

Solipsism – The idea that oneself (or one's consciousness) is the only thing that exists.

Substance Dualism – see *Dualism*.

Thought Experiment – An imaginary situation used to focus attention on and examine an idea or concept.

About the Author

Deborah Wells is a writer, author and the Editor *Iff Books*, the philosophy and science imprint of 'John Hunt Publishing Ltd'. Her previous book, *The Dark Man* (2010) is also published by *O Books*. She lives in Yorkshire, England.

BOOKS

O is a symbol of the world, of oneness and unity. In different cultures it also means the "eye," symbolizing knowledge and insight. We aim to publish books that are accessible, constructive and that challenge accepted opinion, both that of academia and the "moral majority."

Our books are available in all good English language bookstores worldwide. If you don't see the book on the shelves ask the bookstore to order it for you, quoting the ISBN number and title. Alternatively you can order online (all major online retail sites carry our titles) or contact the distributor in the relevant country, listed on the copyright page.

See our website www.o-books.net for a full list of over 500 titles, growing by 100 a year.

And tune in to myspiritradio.com for our book review radio show, hosted by June-Elleni Laine, where you can listen to the authors discussing their books.